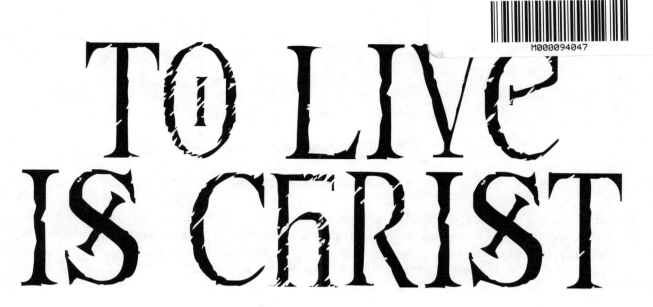

TO LIVE IS CHRIST

The Life and Ministry of Paul

Leader Guide

Beth Moore

LifeWay Press®
Nashville, Tennessee

ISBN 0-7673-3411-6

Dewey Decimal Classification: 248.84
Subject Heading: CHRISTIAN LIFE \ PAUL, APOSTLE

Printed in the United States of America

Leadership and Adult Publishing
LifeWay Church Resources
One LifeWay Plaza
Nashville, TN 37234-0175

Introduction

To Live Is Christ by Beth Moore is an in-depth study of the life and ministry of Paul. Exploring the life of the apostle Paul will:

- deepen our understanding of God's grace;
- demonstrate God's ability to use anyone who is willing to serve Him;
- demonstrate the impact one surrendered life can have;
- encourage us to remain strong and steadfast during times of suffering;
- remind us of the importance of God's Word in the life of every servant;
- demonstrate the power of earnest prayer;
- teach us much of the history of the church in the New Testament;
- benefit us in our relationships with other Christians;
- encourage us to be bolder witnesses for Christ;
- help us become less threatened by death;
- most of all, increase our passion to know Christ!

This guide has been prepared to equip you to plan and lead a study of *To Live Is Christ* for groups in your church or community. You will find administrative guidance, help for planning and promoting the study, and step-by-step instructions for conducting 11 group-study sessions. To prepare adequately, you also need to watch the leadership segment on tape 1 of the videotape series provided in the leader kit. In it author Beth Moore and Chris Adams, Women's Enrichment and Minister's Wives Specialist at LifeWay Christian Resources of the Southern Baptist Convention, discuss additional administrative suggestions for offering this study.

COURSE OVERVIEW

This in-depth course was designed to be completed over 11 weeks through a combination of daily, individual study and weekly group sessions.

Individual study. Each participant needs a copy of the book *To Live Is Christ,* which contains reading assignments interspersed with activities designed to reinforce and apply learning. The member book is divided into an introduction and 10 weeks of content. Every week's material contains 5 daily lessons, each requiring about 45 minutes to complete. Participants complete the daily reading and the learning activities at home in preparation for the weekly group sessions.

Group sessions. Participants meet once each week for a two-hour group session that guides them to discuss and apply what they have learned during their daily, individual study. The small-group portion of this session encourages accountability and allows members to benefit from the insights of other participants as they process the material they have studied during the week. The small groups also help build relationships as participants share prayer concerns and pray together. In the large-group time, members watch weekly video presentations in which Beth Moore enhances the material in the book and concludes each session with additional truths and challenges.

GROUP-SESSION FORMAT

For members to receive maximal benefit from this study, plan for a 2-hour group session each week, plus a 15-minute check-in period. Following this format ensures that members receive the blessings of intimate experiences with God through daily study, support and fellowship through small-group discussions, and inspiration through the video presentations. The session-leadership suggestions in this guide reflect the following schedule, although times shown here are arbitrary selections.

8:45	Child care open, attendance and homework check (15 mins.)
9:00	Large group—welcome, worship, and prayer (15 mins.)
9:15	Small groups (45 mins.) • Prayer (5 mins.) • Discussion of principal questions (20 mins.) • Discussion of personal discussion questions (20 mins.)
10:00	Break and return to large group (5 mins.)
10:05	Large group (55 mins.) • Video presentation (50 mins.) • Closing assignment and prayer (5 mins.)
11:00	Dismiss

This schedule is ideal for a weekday or a weeknight study. It may also be followed for the church's Discipleship Training period if the study is begun an hour early and does not interfere with other church activities.

Some elements of this format may be adjusted to your preferences or needs. For example, you may prefer to add time for a longer break between the small- and large-group periods. Feel free to adjust the schedule, but we encourage you not to omit any one of the three key ingredients of this learning model: (1) individual study of the member book at home, (2) small-group discussion of the principal questions and the personal discussion questions in each week's material in the member book, and (3) large-group viewing of the videos.

Here is an overview of the procedures for each segment of the group session.

Child care open, attendance and homework check (15 mins.). Allow time for mothers to leave their children in child-care facilities before the session begins. Each participant needs to check in and have homework reviewed by the small-group facilitator outside the large-group meeting room before entering. The facilitator does not check for correct responses but simply verifies that each member's work was done.

Large group—welcome, worship, and prayer (15 mins.). The large-group leader is responsible for convening the group and conducting this portion of the session. You may wish to plan special music or select an appropriate hymn or praise song for the group to sing. End this segment with prayer for the day's learning experience.

Small-group discussion (45 mins.). If the number of participants is small, remain in one group for this segment. If you enroll more than 12 people, however, you need to plan for a small group for every 10 to 12 people and enlist a small-group facilitator for each group. These facilitators are responsible for taking prayer requests, having a prayer time (5 mins.), and guiding participants to discuss the principal questions (20 mins.) and personal discussion questions (20 mins.) in each week's material in the member book.

Return to large group (5 mins.). This transitional time allows time for a brief break. Provide light refreshments if desired.

Video presentation (50 mins.). A video presentation by Beth Moore is provided in the leader kit for each week's group session. The large-group leader should play the appropriate video at this time. Participants complete the corresponding video response sheet at the end of each week's material in their member books as they view the video. Beth concludes each video segment with a personal word and an additional challenge.

Closing assignment and prayer (5 mins.). The large-group leader encourages participants to complete the next week's daily assignments and closes with a prayer of praise or thanksgiving.

OPTIONAL FORMAT

A format of 2 hours per week for 10 weeks is ideal for *To Live Is Christ;* however, you may need another option to fit your group's situation. Many groups study these materials with an alternate schedule. The problem with studying on a schedule other than one unit per week is that members do not get into the regular habit of daily Bible study.

If you adopt an alternate plan, please take steps to encourage members to study the Bible daily. If your group can only meet for one hour per week, consider this plan. View the video one week, and conduct the group study the next week. To maintain the continuity of daily study, encourage members to complete the daily work in the member book during the first week. Then, encourage them to review the work daily during the second week. Ask them to write down their answers to the Principal Questions and Personal Discussion Questions each day during their review.

Some groups meet once a month. If your group meets on some schedule other than weekly or bi-weekly, consider using an aid to encourage daily Bible study. One such resource is called *Day By Day in God's Kingdom.* It is a discipleship journal built around six Christian disciplines. It allows disciples to record their spiritual journeys as they study courses such as *To Live Is Christ.* Ask your members to complete the work in *To Live Is Christ* during the first week of the month and to review the material the week before the group meets.

In *To Live Is Christ,* you will read most of the Book of Acts, the prison epistles, and the letters to Timothy and Titus. If your group meets on an extended schedule, you may want to develop a schedule for members to read Romans, 1 and 2 Corinthians, Galatians, and 1 and 2 Thessalonians as part of their daily study.

RESOURCES

These resources are available for leaders and participants.

- *To Live Is Christ* (member book) is an interactive workbook by Beth Moore providing an introduction and 10 weeks of daily, biblical studies on the life and ministry of Paul. The book also includes response sheets to be completed as participants view the video segments in the weekly group sessions. Each participant needs a copy of the member book. Order item 0-7673-3412-4.
- *To Live Is Christ Leader Kit* contains one copy of the book *To Live Is Christ;* this leader guide; and six videotapes. Five of the videotapes feature 10 lectures in which Beth Moore teaches material related to the content of the book. A sixth video provides

content for an introductory group session, administrative guidance for organizing and leading the study, and a brief promotion/enlistment segment that includes a 30-second spot for use on local television stations. These videos are provided in the leader kit and are not available separately. Order item 0-7673-3402-7.

- *To Live Is Christ Leader Guide* offers easy-to-follow, step-by-step directions for facilitating 11 group sessions, using *To Live Is Christ* and the videotapes included in the leader kit. This guide, one copy of which is included in the leader kit, is available separately. Order item 0-7673-3411-6.
- *To Live Is Christ Audiotapes* include the audio portions of Beth Moore's video presentations on 6 cassette tapes, with a 16-page listening guide. Although the tapes were designed for individual study, a leader may wish to use them for personal review and inspiration. Order item 0-7673-2995-3.

You will also need the following materials.

- Registration tables
- Small signs that indicate divisions of the alphabet—A–E, F–J, K–O, P–S, T–Z, for example.
- Registration cards
- An attendance sheet for each small-group facilitator
- Name tags
- Pencils
- Bibles
- A videotape player and monitor

CHOOSING LEADERS

The following are descriptions of the roles and responsibilities of leaders.

Large-group leader. This leader is not a teacher but an organizer, coordinator, and facilitator. The large-group leader's responsibilities include—

- providing administrative leadership for the group;
- scheduling the study;
- promoting the study and coordinating enrollment efforts;
- enlisting and coordinating the work of small-group facilitators;
- ordering and distributing resources;
- maintaining and submitting accurate records of participation each week as Discipleship Training attendance;
- leading the large-group segments of the weekly group sessions.

The large-group leader should be someone who is interested in exploring the crucial truths of this course and who desires to help others grow in intimacy with God. A long list of qualifications and years of teaching experience are not required. A heart prepared by God—being available and teachable—is more important. Paramount to this leader's success is a strong commitment to study of this course and a faithful fulfillment of the basic responsibilities of group leadership.

This leader guide provides the large-group leader administrative help for organizing a Bible study group. It also gives specific guidance to prepare for and lead 11 group sessions.

Small-group facilitators. Enlist a small-group facilitator for every 10 to 12 participants. Again, these are not teachers but facilitators of the small groups' discussion and fellowship. Their responsibilities include—

- greeting and registering participants at the introductory session;
- calling members assigned to their small groups after the introductory session to introduce themselves, to tell them the locations of their small-group meeting rooms, and to encourage them to complete the daily assignments in week 1 of the member book;
- checking small-group members' attendance and homework prior to each week's meeting;
- taking prayer requests, conducting a prayer time at the beginning of the small-group period, praying for participants, and encouraging participants to pray for one another;
- guiding members to discuss the principal questions (listed at the beginning of each week's material in the member book) and the personal discussion questions (designated by a scroll in the member book);
- promoting fellowship among group members;
- noting opportunities for follow-up ministry.

If you have 12 or fewer participants, one leader can serve both the large and small-group function. Each session of this guide designates the point during the session when small-group discussion is to occur. Share with each small-group facilitator a list of responsibilities and the following information about facilitating and handling problems in small groups.

FACILITATING SMALL-GROUP DISCUSSION

You will find many applications in this study for a contemporary walk with God. Beth Moore applies many of the course's concepts in her video presentations. In addition, the member book encourages participants to apply what they are learning as they complete their daily assignments.

One purpose of the small-group discussion period each week is to enable members to make meaningful application to their daily lives. Small-group facilitators will guide discussions of each week's principal questions, listed at the beginning of each week's material in the member book, as well as the personal discussion questions indicated by 📜 in each day's lesson. Small-group facilitators can use the following guidelines to make these discussion times effective in challenging participants spiritually and promoting life change.

- Arrange the chairs in the meeting room in a circle or a semicircle so that participants can see one another. Seating should not physically exclude anyone.
- Greet group members as they arrive and start the meeting on time. Allow 5 minutes for participants to share prayer requests; then pray or ask a participant to pray. Make notes when prayer requests are shared. Assure members that you are concerned not only about their spiritual growth but also about their personal lives. Encourage them to pray for one another during the week. If someone is experiencing difficult circumstances, write a note or call between sessions to say that you are praying for her and that you care.
- Spend 20 minutes discussing the week's principal questions (listed at the beginning of the week's material in the member book) and 20 minutes discussing personal discussion questions (designated by a scroll + in the member book). Emphasize that only participants who wish to respond should do so; no one is required to share responses. Do not force the discussion questions on members. Adapt and change them as necessary. Be flexible if members wish to spend more time on one group of questions or if they raise specific issues. Be sensitive to members' particular needs as the discussion progresses. Remember that your job is not to teach the material but to encourage and lead participants in sharing their insights about the work they have done during the week and in applying the content to their spiritual journeys.
- Be personally involved without relinquishing leadership. Your role as facilitator is that of a fellow disciple—one who shares the same struggles the other participants have in their spiritual lives. You need to be emotionally vulnerable and willing to share some of your own feelings and responses. However, you must also recognize that someone must lead the group and direct the discussion at all times. Be flexible but do not allow the discussion to veer off on a tangent. Keep the focus on the week's content and its application.
- Try to create a relaxed atmosphere that will help every member feel a sense of belonging. Use first names. Do not rush the discussion.
- Pray for the Holy Spirit's leadership; then allow Him freedom to direct the session as He wills. His movement may be evident in tears of joy or conviction, emotional or spiritual brokenness, or the thrill of a newfound insight. Be sensitive to signs of God's work in a person's life and follow up by asking the person to share. Giving participants the opportunity to testify to what God is doing is very important. Often, the testimony may help another person with a similar issue. Follow the Holy Spirit's leadership as God works in these discussion times.
- Be sure that you do not talk too much as facilitator. Do not be afraid of periods of silence.
- Be an encourager. Show a caring, loving spirit. Communicate acceptance and concern. Especially if your group includes non-Christians, you need to create an atmosphere that communicates, "I accept you as you are." Accepting participants does not necessarily mean that you agree with their values or choices. You can love a person without agreeing with that person. If a participant shares something that makes her feel vulnerable or ashamed, say something like: "I know your sharing took a lot of courage. I admire you for being willing to share it."
- Listen intently and aggressively. When someone shares something personal or painful, lean toward her. Use facial expressions to show concern. Nod your head.
- Be ready to address special needs that members may reveal. If someone is unsaved, follow the Holy Spirit's leadership to know the right time to talk with the person privately to lead her to Christ. If a participant reveals emotional pain or family problems, assure her of the group's concern and support and pause briefly to pray with the person. Then offer to meet with her later to help her find additional help if needed.
- Set boundaries. Do not permit a group member to act in a verbally abusive way toward another member. Do not force group members to do or say anything they are not willing to do or say. Try gently nudging a group member to a point of discovery and growth instead of pushing her to a conclusion for which she is not ready.
- Be enthusiastic!

• End the discussion period on time. You will face a challenge each week in bringing the discussion to an end in time for members to have a five-minute break before the large group reconvenes. At the first session emphasize the need to conclude on time each week. A few minutes before the time to end the discussion period, help the person speaking reach a point of closure. Then ask if anyone else has anything to add. Take time to respond, but at some point cut off the discussion. If someone is not finished, affirm the importance of what the person is saying. Offer to continue the discussion next week and ask that member to introduce the topic at the beginning of the next meeting. Or you may need to spend time privately with the person if the topic does not relate to the entire group. Be sure you have tied loose ends. Did you put someone on hold during the discussion? Did you get back to the person? Was someone's sharing interrupted as you moved to focus on someone else's response? Did you reach closure with the original speaker? Finally, remind group members to pray for one another during the week.

COPING WITH PROBLEMS IN THE SMALL GROUP

No matter how meaningful the study and how effective the leadership, difficulties can arise in any group. Following are common problems and suggestions for dealing with them.

Absenteeism. Absentees miss a potentially life-changing experience and diminish others' learning. If a participant is absent, contact the person, communicate your concern, and encourage her to make up the work. Otherwise, a participant will quickly get further behind and likely drop out.

Not completing at-home assignments. Emphasize in the introductory session that a significant course requirement is doing daily study at home, including completion of the learning activities. State that each person's book will be checked before each session to see that homework was completed. Anyone who is not willing to make this commitment should not participate in the study.

If someone has not completed the week's assignments, encourage the person to stay up-to-date to gain the greatest benefits from the study. If someone continually refuses to complete the assignments, meet with her and suggest that she withdraw and participate at a time when she can devote herself adequately to the study.

Disagreement with the content. Some debate in a group is productive. Remember that the Scriptures should always be the final source of authority. If debate becomes counterproductive, suggest that you and the participant discuss the matter later so other members can participate in the present discussion.

Do not feel threatened if someone expects you to be an authority and to answer all of her questions. Emphasize your role as the facilitator of the discussion, pointing out that participants are to learn from one another and that you are not an authority on the subject. Suggest that a volunteer research the question during the week and report at the next meeting if the person insists that an answer is important to her.

A participant who dominates the group. Ways a person may dominate a group are—
• claiming a major portion of each discussion period to talk about her issues;
• repeatedly waiting until the last 10 minutes of a meeting to introduce an emotionally charged story or problem;
• attempting to block other group members' sharing;
• judging others' behavior or confessions;
• challenging your leadership in a hostile way;
• criticizing other group members' motives or feelings.

As the facilitator, make sure every person has an opportunity to share. Discourage dominating members by calling on others, by asking someone to speak who has not yet responded, or by focusing directly on someone else. If these methods do not work, talk privately with the dominating person and enlist the person's support in involving everyone in future discussions.

When a person is going into too much detail and is losing the attention of the group, you will usually notice that the group has disconnected. Direct the sharing back on course by discreetly interrupting the person and by restating the point she is trying to make: "So what you are saying is …." Another method is to interrupt and restate the question you asked originally: "And Liz, what did you learn about God's love through that experience?" Even if the speaker is somewhat unsettled by this response, she should respond by restating the response more succinctly.

PLANNING STEPS

The following steps are suggested to assist the large-group leader in organizing a study of *To Live Is Christ.*
1. Enlist the support of your pastor. His endorsement will encourage people to deepen their spiritual lives. Perhaps he will agree to announce from the pulpit this discipleship opportunity for members.
2. Talk with the likely participants of your church to determine the level of interest in this type of in-

depth study. Also ask whether the study should be offered during the day, in the evening, or both. When scheduling the study, be sensitive to the needs of women who work outside the home.

3. Schedule 11 weeks on the church calender that will allow the greatest participation. Fall and spring studies usually result in more participation than summer sessions do. However, summertime may afford some persons with seasonal careers, such as schoolteachers, an opportunity to attend an intimate discipleship study.

4. Offer child care if possible. This provision will increase your attendance and ensure greater weekly participation.

5. If possible allow two hours for each weekly session. This time period will allow ample opportunities for both weekly activities: small-group discussion of the participants' home study and large-group viewing of the week's video presentation.

6. After estimating the number of participants, order member books (*To Live Is Christ,* item 0-7673-3412-4) between four and six weeks in advance by writing to LifeWay Church Resources Customer Service; One LifeWay Plaza; Nashville, TN 37234-0113; by sending a fax to (615) 251-5933; by calling 1-800-458-2772; by emailing *customerservice@lifeway.com* or by visiting the Lifeway Christian Store serving you. Decide whether the church will pay for member books or whether participants will pay for their own. Experience has shown that if members pay for their books or a portion of the cost, they are likely to make a more serious commitment to the study. Make sure that scholarships are provided for members who cannot afford to purchase their own books.

7. Find a meeting room that will accommodate your large-group sessions and reserve it for the duration of the study. Also reserve small-group meeting rooms for the number of groups you will have. Arrange the meeting rooms to be as intimate as possible. Chairs in the small-group rooms should be arranged in circles or semicircles. Semicircular rows of chairs are acceptable for the large-group room as long as all participants can view the video.

8. Conduct a planning session for the large-group leader and the small-group facilitators. Complete the following actions in the meeting.
   • Obtain copies of this leader guide for your small-group facilitators. Discuss the group-session format and their responsibilities, which include:
     —greeting and registering participants at the introductory session;
     —calling members assigned to their small groups after the introductory session to introduce themselves, to tell them the locations of their small-group meeting rooms, and to encourage them to complete the daily assignments in week 1 of the member book;
     —checking small-group members' attendance and homework prior to each week's meeting;
     —taking prayer requests, conducting a prayer time at the beginning of the small-group period, praying for participants, and encouraging participants to pray for one another;
     —guiding members to discuss the principal questions (listed at the beginning of each week's material in the member book) and the personal discussion questions (designated by a scroll);
     —promoting fellowship among group members;
     —noting opportunities for follow-up ministry.
   • View the administrative segment on tape 1 of the video series provided in the leader kit.
   • Discuss registration procedures. Plan to set up several registration tables outside the large-group meeting room with signs indicating divisions of the alphabet. For example, participants whose last names begin with A–E will register at one station, F–J at the next, K–O at the next, P–S at the next, and T–Z at the final station. Assign small-group facilitators to handle registration at the stations. The members registered by a particular facilitator would become members of her group. Make adjustments if numbers fall unevenly. Instruct the facilitators to be at their stations 30 minutes before registration begins at the introductory session. Provide them with a supply of member books, registration cards, pencils, and reusable name tags. Tell each registrar that she has the responsibility of making a good first impression. She needs to wear a name tag, greet members with enthusiasm, answer their questions as best she can or promise to find out the answers, make them feel welcome, and direct them to the large-group session. At subsequent sessions the small-group facilitators will follow the same procedures to check attendance and homework.
   • Explain that after the introductory session small-group facilitators will transfer names from their registration cards to attendance sheets that you will provide. Each week they will record attendance, completion of homework, and prayer requests on this sheet. Emphasize that facilitators are merely to check whether participants have responded to the

learning activities in the member book, not to determine whether responses are correct.

9. Promote the study, using the suggestions in the following section.

10. Plan to keep accurate records and report attendance to the church office. Regardless of when the study is offered, it is a Discipleship Training study and should be reported as Discipleship Training participation on the Annual Church Profile. Another reason to keep accurate participation records is that participants can earn Christian Growth Study Plan diplomas for completing the study. For details see the requirements on page 223 of the member book.

11. Pray, pray, and keep praying that God will involve the members He desires and that He will validate this study with His obvious presence and activity!

PROMOTING THE STUDY

This study provides a wonderful opportunity for outreach because it is free of rules and does not require a particular church affiliation. Target persons in your community who are interested in Bible study. Church bulletins, newsletters, handouts, posters, fliers at Mothers' Day Out, announcements in worship services and in Sunday School classes, phone calls, and word of mouth are excellent and inexpensive ways to promote the study. Sometimes local radio and television stations announce upcoming events free of charge.

To assist you in promoting the study, we have provided two special promotional segments on tape 1 of the videos included in the leader kit. You may want to preview them now. You will find them immediately after the administrative segment and immediately before the introductory session. The first segment has been designed for your use inside the church—in a worship service, in a women's Bible study class, and in other locations where women regularly gather during the week. You have permission to duplicate this segment if you wish to create a loop tape that plays continually. Be sure to have someone prepared to announce the date, time, and place of the introductory session and to invite persons to attend. If the tape is left to play unattended, place a sign beside the monitor that lists the date, time, and place of the introductory session.

The second promotional segment is a 30-second commercial that can be used on a local television station or cable channel. We have left a blank screen for the last few seconds so that you can have the television station or cable company insert your personal invitation on the screen. Again, you have permission to duplicate this commercial as needed. If you would like a broadcast-quality copy of either the longer promotional segment or the television commercial, you may order one for a nominal fee by calling Lee Sizemore at (615) 251-2882. Allow between two and three weeks for duplication and delivery.

Notes

_____

_____

_____

_____

_____

_____

_____

Introductory Session

GOALS FOR THIS SESSION

In this session you will—
- register all members for *To Live Is Christ;*
- develop a role or attendance sheet;
- distribute member books;
- welcome all members in joint session;
- explain basics about the format in joint session;
- view introductory video presentation.

BEFORE THE SESSION

1. If you are expecting 20 or more participants, set up tables in the designated meeting room with cards indicating a division of the alphabet at several stations. For example, those with last names beginning with letters A–E will sign up at one station, F–J at the next, etc.

2. Enlist a volunteer or group leader to sit at each station. One way of distributing members to groups is to designate those each leader registers as members of her group. Adjustments will need to be made where numbers fall unevenly.

3. Each "registrar," whether leader or volunteer, should be at her station 30 minutes before registration is to begin. Each should be equipped with member books, registration cards or sign-up sheets (drawn up by your church or study leader), pens, and name tags.

4. Each registrar assumes the responsibility for the first impression of each new member. She needs to wear her name tag, be ready to greet new members with enthusiasm, anticipate questions with knowledgeable answers, make them feel welcome, and tell them what to do next. (After registration, members will report to joint session for the introductory session only. After this first introductory meeting, members will begin each week in their large groups for welcome, worship and prayer.)

DURING THE SESSION

Introduction to *To Live Is Christ* (60 mins.)

1. Open introductory session in prayer.
2. Welcome members and introduce leadership. If your group is small, you might have each member introduce herself. You may want to create your own icebreaker to help introduce members to one another.

3. After introductions, the leader should give instructions and information concerning the course. This information will include the following and any additional points pertinent to your church facility:

A. Have members scan the first week's daily assignments. Make sure they understand that a week of study is to be completed prior to each weekly meeting. Before your next meeting, week 1 should be complete. Make sure they understand that, although the daily assignments are absolutely crucial to the course, members are still urged to attend the weekly sessions even if their work is incomplete. Tell them to expect each daily assignment to take approximately 30–45 minutes.

B. Encourage members to read the introduction in the member book before beginning their study.

C. Using the introduction to the member book, explain that the format and distinctive features of the book were designed to enhance learning. Point out that the Principal Questions, listed in the introduction to each unit, and the Personal Discussion Questions, designated by a scroll, will be discussed in the weekly group sessions.

D. Emphasize the primary reasons for small-group discussion are:
- to practice accountability—in-depth Bible studies are most often completed successfully in a group.
- to underscore the basic biblical truths that have been disclosed the previous week. This will be accomplished through discussing answers to the Principal Questions, which insure that the biblical information offered in the study has been received and understood.
- to see ways in which this study can be personally applied. This will be accomplished through discussing answers to the Personal Discussion Questions (marked with a scroll).

E. Express the extreme need to be good stewards of the time given for each session. The way time is organized can mean the success or failure of any group. Ask them to adopt the following time guidelines for the remaining sessions.
- Leaders: Be early!
- Members: Be on time!
- Small groups: Start on time! Leaders must make

a habit from the beginning to start on time regardless of the number present.

- Members: Your personal comments are vital to the discussion time, but please make them brief and to the point in order to make the class run smoothly.

4. After today's introductory meeting, members will participate in a small group each week as well as a large group. (Tell them they will receive a phone call within 24 hours identifying their leader and telling them where their group will meet for discussion of sessions 1—10.) Allow 45 minutes for small-group discussion divided according to the following schedule.

- Prayer requests and prayer (5 mins.). If you ask for prayer requests, ask that they be stated in one brief sentence. Be prepared to graciously intervene if a request becomes lengthy.
- Discussion of the Principal Questions and Personal Discussion Questions (40 mins.). Allow 7–8 minutes to discuss each day's assignment. Each day's Principal Questions can be answered in 2–3 minutes leaving 5–6 minutes for Personal Discussion Questions. Write these time divisions on a chalkboard for all members to keep in mind and be dedicated to enforcing them.

Introductory Video Presentation (50 mins.)

After group discussion, gather members in joint session to view the video which enhances and then concludes each unit. Take only 5 minutes for the transition between group discussion and video presentation. The video presentation will be 45–50 minutes.

Closing Remarks and Prayer (5 mins.)

1. After viewing the video, share any closing comments. Give a brief introduction to the next unit. This introduction may be as simple as saying, "This week we'll consider Paul's early life as the son of a Pharisee."

2. Answer any questions, or if you do not know the answer, call the questioner as soon as you have the information she desires. Don't forget to take up name tags as the group departs.

AFTER THE SESSION

1. Compile all registration cards or lists and, if there are more than 12 members and more than 1 leader, divide the list of members into small groups. These discussion groups ideally need to be a maximum of 12 members.

2. Have leader(s) call members within the next 24 hours to introduce themselves and tell them where their group will meet the following week.

3. Have a leader or volunteer create attendance sheets from the registration cards so that every leader will be able to take role of her individual group at each of the next 10 sessions. These attendance sheets need to be given to each leader prior to the next session.

I know you can do it. If you follow these guidelines you will have no problem being good stewards of the 2-hour time period. As a leader, you can help insure learners are receiving the utmost from this study by implementing the suggestions you've received through this introduction.

Before we proceed to the instructions for sessions 1—10, I would like to express one last thing to you. As a leader of *To Live Is Christ* you have the opportunity to witness lives being changed, not the least of which is your own! How can I say this having no idea how this Bible study will be received in your church? Because God's Word changes lives! If a woman dedicates herself to the hours in God's Word this study will require, her life is undoubtedly going to be transformed. As a leader, be careful not to let your administration of this study eclipse your participation. Open God's Word and enjoy! Walk in faith toward the woman He's designed you to become. His Word will not return void!

Notes

_____

_____

_____

_____

SESSION 1
The First Footprints

BEFORE THE SESSION

1. Complete all of week 1 in the member book.
2. Pause and pray for each member of your group by name. Pray specifically that each will be teachable and that God will reveal Himself to her through this Bible study.
3. Pray for God's guidance in your preparation for this week's group session.
4. Carefully read through "During the Session" and make sure you are prepared for each question and activity that will take place at this week's group session.
5. Arrange your room to meet the needs of your group. An intimate setting seems to be most beneficial. If you have a group of 12 or under, arrange the chairs in a tight circle. If you have more than 12, two tight semicircles will work well.
6. If you are using the video, do the following:
   - Make sure all arrangements have been made to secure and set up necessary equipment.
   - If you have more than one small group, the arrangements need to be made in one room for the joint session. If you have only one group, the arrangements will be made in the room where the discussion group meets.
   - Preview the video and fill in your viewing guide. This step will be beneficial to you in case you are detained or distracted with administrative duties as the members watch the video.
   - Prepare several sentences based on your response to the video from which you can make closing remarks at the end of class just prior to dismissal.

Child Care Open, Attendance and Homework Check (15 mins.)

DURING THE SESSION

Large Group—Welcome, Worship, and Prayer (15 mins.)

1. Greet each member as she arrives and give her the name tag she used in the introductory session. Learn to call every participant by name.
2. Lead a time of worship and praise.
3. Pray, asking for God's presence and blessing throughout the session.
4. Dismiss to small groups.

Small Groups (45 mins.)

1. Ask for prayer requests and have prayer. (5 mins.)
2. Review the Week's Principal Questions and Personal Discussion Questions (40 mins.)

Look for brief and basic answers to the principal questions just so you can be satisfied that the material was received and understood, 2–3 minutes should be sufficient. All answers should be obvious as the reading and the learning activities of week 1 are performed and completed; however, make sure that you have written basic answers to the questions so that you can supply the information if a member does not volunteer or understand the answer.

Each day's Principal Question will be followed by a Personal Discussion Question. These questions are identified in each day's study by a scroll. The Personal Discussion Questions can be answered by anyone who feels comfortable sharing. Group members should feel no pressure to share their personal answers but should be given the opportunity if they wish. Please ask them always to be discreet and never to name another person who could be hurt by the discussion. Appropriate discussion of these questions will be invaluable to the application of the session. Leader, you must be ready and willing to redirect discussion if at any point it becomes inappropriate. Please pray for discretion and boldness on your part.

Day 1:
- *Principal Question:* How would you describe the events surrounding the circumcision of an infant boy in an ancient Hebrew home?
- *Personal Discussion:* Based on what you've read today, in what ways is a typical orthodox Jewish home of Paul's generation like a Christian home of our generation? How is it different?

Day 2:
- *Principal Question:* What are a few ways the ancient Hebrew home emphasized Scripture in the life of a young boy?
- *Personal Discussion:* We don't practice the outward expression of the Jew, but we are wise to share the inward principle. How has God's Word been a shield of protection in a time of weakness for you?

Day 3:
- *Principal Question:* How would you describe Gamaliel, Saul's primary teacher in Jerusalem?
- *Personal Discussion:* Several wonderful Psalms help sketch vivid mental images of the ancient Jew's Jerusalem. Read Psalm 48:1-14 and Psalm 122:3-4 carefully. Use their descriptions to create a brief paragraph young Saul might have written to his best friend in Tarsus after seeing the city.

Day 4:
- *Principal Question:* What would you imagine Paul's life was like as he attempted to live faultlessly by the law?
- *Personal Discussion:* Have you been there? I have! Trying to obey and serve Him before we've come to love Him can be exhausting. Has your attempt to serve God or be good for God's sake ever exceeded your love for God? If so, describe how you felt or what happened as a result.

Day 5:
- *Principal Question:* What important event occurred in Jerusalem in the years following Saul's assumed departure?
- *Personal Discussion:* Describe a way the enemy has tried to tempt you with self-interest so you would reject the purposes of God in your life.

If time allows, ask what ways God spoke directly to members in week 1.

Conclude 40-minute discussion time by thanking members for their willingness to share and affirming their apparent grasp of the material. If you are using the optional video, it is time to move into large group to view the video or turn on the video in the one small group. If you are not viewing the video, you may dismiss with a few introductory words about week 2 and a closing prayer at this time. Take the 5 remaining minutes in the first hour to prepare for the video.

Break and return to large group (5 mins.)

View the Video Presentation (50 mins.)

Conclude Session (5 mins.)
- Leader gives a brief response to the video in one or two sentences.
- Leader gives a brief introduction to week 2 in her own words and encourages them to complete the next week's study before the next session.

- Leader closes with prayer. This would not be the time to take prayer requests. That opportunity was given at the beginning of the small-group session.
- Leader takes up name tags as group departs.

If you were able to abide by your time schedule, you will be able to dismiss on time. However, satisfy any unexpected, but brief, needs or comments that arise.

AFTER THE SESSION
1. Immediately record any concerns or impressions you had to pray for any member in your group while it is still fresh on your mind. Remember to pray for these throughout the week.
2. Evaluate session 1 by asking yourself the following questions and recording your answers:
   - Was I adequately prepared for today's session?
   - Was I able to begin and end session 1 on time?
   - If not, how can I help to make sure our time is used more wisely in session 2?
   - Do any members need extra encouragement this week? Note whether a card or a phone call would be appropriate; then, remember to follow up on each one.
   - What was my overall impression of session 1?
3. Read through "Before the Session" on page 12 so that you will know what preparations you'll need to make before your next session.
4. Have lunch with a friend, stop for a soft drink, have a cup of hot chocolate, or make time for a nap. Treat yourself to a moment's recreation for the work you've allowed God to accomplish through you!

JUST BETWEEN US

The first session is behind you, and you're on your way to an exciting adventure with Paul. I know you're going to be a great leader, but I also don't want you to miss a single blessing as a participant in this journey. Don't let the details distract you. Enjoy your group! God has handpicked each one of your participants. They will be more blessed by your joy than your skill. As you give God your hands to serve Him diligently, don't forget to give Him your heart. Be the first among your group members to allow God to do something glorious. He handpicked you, too. I believe He has a special work He wants to do in your life. May God make Himself "visible" in you!

S E S S I O N   2
Finding the Way

BEFORE THE SESSION
Refer to page 12 for a description of session procedures.

Child Care Open, Attendance and Homework Check (15 mins.)

DURING THE SESSION
Large Group—Welcome, Worship, and Prayer (15 mins.)
1. Greet each member as she arrives and give her the name tag she used in the introductory session. Learn to call every participant by name.
2. Lead a time of worship and praise.
3. Pray, asking for God's presence and blessing throughout the session.
4. Dismiss to small groups.

Small Groups (45 mins.)
1. Ask for prayer requests and have prayer. (5 mins.)
2. Review the Week's Principal Questions and Personal Discussion Questions (40 mins.)

Remember, Leader, you are looking for brief and basic answers to the Principal Questions that will indicate the comprehension of the reading and learning activities in week 2. Again, make sure that you are prepared to offer the answer in the event that a member does not volunteer. Also, be prepared to keep personal discussion within appropriate bounds.

Day 1:
- *Principal Question:* What was the connection and contrast between Saul and Stephen?
- *Personal Discussion:* What are several important advantages to forgiving your persecutors? Briefly describe an experience when you found forgiving difficult.

Day 2:
- *Principal Question:* What was most significant to you about Saul's conversion?
- *Personal Discussion:* Can you think of a person whose public testimony of God's forgiveness helped you to finally accept it yourself? Explain briefly.

Day 3:
- *Principal Question:* When Saul set out to prove to the Jews that Jesus was the Christ, what method did he use?
- *Personal Discussion:* Reflect for a moment on your Christian life. Who has been a Barnabas to you and how did he or she encourage you?

Day 4:
- *Principal Question:* How did God speak to Peter about prejudice?
- *Personal Discussion:* Have you ever taken an unpopular stand against prejudice? If so, explain briefly.

Day 5:
- *Principal Question:* How did Barnabas and Saul begin their ministry together?
- *Personal Discussion:* Can you think of a way your belief was characterized by a turn?

If time allows, ask what ways God spoke directly to members in week 2.

Conclude the 40-minute discussion time by affirming your members in their participation today and their apparent grasp of the material. If you are using the video, move into large group to view the video or turn on the video in the one small group. If you are not viewing the video, you may dismiss with a few introductory words about week 3 and a closing prayer.

Break and return to large group (5 mins.)

View the Video Presentation (50 mins.)

Conclude Session (5 mins.)
- Leader gives a brief response to the video in one or two sentences.
- Leader gives a brief introduction to week 3 in her own words and encourages them toward the completion of their home study.
- Leader closes with prayer. Again, prayer requests will not be necessary since they were taken at the beginning of discussion.
- Leader takes up name tags as group departs.

AFTER THE SESSION

1. Immediately record any concerns or impressions you had to pray for any member in your group while it is still fresh on your mind. Remember to pray for these throughout the week.

2. Evaluate session 2 by asking yourself the following questions. Be sure to record your answers.

   - Was I adequately prepared for today's session?
   - Was I able to begin and end session 2 on time? If not, how can I make sure our time is used more wisely in session 3?
   - Are there any members that may need extra encouragement this week? Note whether a card or phone call would be appropriate; then, remember to follow up on each one.
   - What was my overall impression of session 2?

3. Read through "Before the Session" on page 12 so that you will know what preparations you'll need to make before your next session.

JUST BETWEEN US

You're doing a wonderful job! I hope you're settling in to your role as leader so you can begin to enjoy yourself. God is using you whether or not you realize it. You have given your time and efforts to a God who never wastes willingness. As you encourage your group members, let God encourage you. He has appointed you as surely as He appointed Ananias. You are His ambassador in your group. Even when you feel like you don't know what you're doing, He knows what He's doing! He commissioned you for this task. He will enable you to fulfill it. Bask in His favor today.

Notes

_____

_____

_____

_____

_____

_____

_____

_____

_____

_____

_____

_____

_____

SESSION 3
Miles and Missions

BEFORE THE SESSION
Refer to page 12 for a description of session procedures.

Child Care Open, Attendance and Homework Check (15 mins.)

DURING THE SESSION
Large Group—Welcome, Worship, and Prayer (15 mins.)
1. Greet each member as she arrives and give her the name tag she used in the introductory session. Learn to call every participant by name.
2. Lead a time of worship and praise.
3. Pray, asking for God's presence and blessing throughout the session.
4. Dismiss to small groups.

Small Groups (45 mins.)
1. Ask for prayer requests and have prayer. (5 mins.)
2. Review the Week's Principal Questions and Personal Discussion Questions (40 mins.)

Day 1:
- *Principal Question:* Who was Bar-Jesus?
- *Personal Discussion:* Look back at the three phases that describe Satan and his servants. Have you seen a recent example of the devil's deceit, trickery, or perversion of God's ways? If so, describe briefly.

Day 2:
- *Principal Question:* What does "being appointed for eternal life" mean?
- *Personal Discussion:* Meditate on the last seven days for several moments. Picture yourself in your usual roles as well as specific encounters. List ways in which you exerted the power of influence whether rightly or wrongly. I will get you started with a few questions I am asking myself: Did you influence your spouse in a decision at work? Did you influence a friend who was upset with someone? Did you influence a class or a group of people in a meeting? Did you influence your boss or employees? Did you influence your children in situations they were in? List every point of influence you can remember, and then add to the list as the Holy Spirit reminds you of others.

Day 3:
- *Principal Question:* Why was Paul stoned?
- *Personal Discussion:* Conclude your lesson by writing a brief testimony of a time God used a difficult situation to draw you with loving kindness to Himself.

Day 4:
- *Principal Question:* How were the Gentiles who were turning to Christ being wrongly burdened?
- *Personal Discussion:* Why would elderly men and women be able to provide unique strength and encouragement to their congregations?

Day 5:
- *Principal Question:* How does Acts 14:21-22 refute many popular prosperity gospels?
- *Personal Discussion:* Let's pause a moment and let God expose any areas where we have tried to make our personal experience a standard for another believer. Try to think in fairly broad terms such as the areas of salvation, spiritual gifts, prayers, miracles, or healings. Any reflections?

If time allows, ask what ways God spoke directly to members in week 3.

Conclude 40-minute discussion time by affirming your members in their participation today and their apparent grasp of the material. If you are using the optional video, move into large group to view the video or turn on the video in the one small group. If you are not viewing the video, you may dismiss with a few introductory words about week 4 and a closing prayer.

Break and return to large group (5 mins.)

View the Video Presentation (50 mins.)

Conclude Session (5 mins.)
- Leader gives a brief response to the video in one or two sentences.
- Leader gives a brief introduction to week 4 in her own words and encourages them toward the completion of their home study.
- Leader closes with prayer. Again, since prayer

requests were taken at the beginning of discussion, they would not be necessary at this time.
- Leader takes up name tags as group departs.

AFTER THE SESSION

1. Immediately record any concerns or impressions you had to pray for any member in your group while it is still fresh on your mind. Remember to pray for these throughout the week.
2. Evaluate session 3 by asking yourself the following questions and recording your answers:
    - Was I adequately prepared for today's session?
    - Was I able to begin and end session 3 on time?
    - If not, how can I help to make sure our time is used more wisely in session 4?
    - Are there any members that may need extra encouragement this week? Note whether a card or phone call would be appropriate; then, remember to follow up on each one.
    - What was my overall impression of session 3?

3. Read through "Before the Session" on page 12 so that you will know what preparations you'll need to make before your next session.

JUST BETWEEN US

I hope you're beginning to sense a growing trust and unity in your group. I'm praying for God to give you wisdom and discernment at times when uncomfortable moments arise. Remember, as the group leader, you will likely be more sensitive to comments, questions, or glitches than the others. Relax in your role and don't feel like you need to know all the answers or perform a certain role perfectly. Just ask God to fill you with the fruit of His Spirit just as we learned in session 3. His personality will permeate your words and expressions. He will use you to help create an atmosphere of love and acceptance. We want everyone in our group to feel accepted even if her beliefs or attitudes are hard to accept. Lead the members in edifying the body of Christ and they will quickly follow. You're doing a great job!

Notes

_____

_____

_____

_____

_____

_____

_____

_____

_____

_____

S E S S I O N   4
Unexpected Sojourners and Wider Paths

BEFORE THE SESSION

Refer to page 12 for a description of session procedures.

Child Care Open, Attendance and Homework Check (15 mins.)

DURING THE SESSION

Large Group—Welcome, Worship, and Prayer (15 mins.)

1. Greet each member as she arrives and give her the name tag she used in the introductory session. Learn to call every participant by name.
2. Lead a time of worship and praise.
3. Pray, asking for God's presence and blessing throughout the session.
4. Dismiss to small groups.

Small Groups (45 mins.)

1. Ask for prayer requests and have prayer. (5 mins.)
2. Review the Week's Principal Questions and Personal Discussion Questions (40 mins.)

Day 1:
- *Principal Question:* Why did Paul and Barnabas go their separate ways?
- *Personal Discussion:* Describe an occasion from your experience when God divided so He could multiply.

Day 2:
- *Principal Question:* How would you describe Timothy?
- *Personal Discussion:* Diagram your heritage of faith on the family tree. You may have a heritage of faith from both parents. You may have a heritage of faith from one side of your family. Or you may be the first believer in several generations. Paul considered Timothy to be his son in the faith even though he was not his biological father. You've probably received a heritage of faith from a spiritual if not a natural mother or father. Find out who gave your spiritual parent his/her heritage of faith. Try to diagram at least three generations on the family tree in your book.

Day 3:
- *Principal Question:* How can we be best equipped to discern God's redirection in our lives?
- *Personal Discussion:* Has God ever redirected you away from a plan you formerly thought was His?

Day 4:
- *Principal Question:* How did God use the imprisonment of Silas and Paul for His glory?
- *Personal Discussion:* What about you? Have you been freed from chains which bound you in the past? If so do you believe God has freed you to leave or freed you to stay? Explain briefly.

Day 5:
- *Principal Question:* Why were the Bereans of more noble character than the Thessalonians?
- *Personal Discussion:* What is at least one Scripture or biblical concept you've nailed down that has kept you from toppling when everything around you seemed to rock?

If time allows, ask what ways God spoke directly to members in week 4.

Conclude 40-minute discussion time by affirming your members in their participation today and their apparent grasp of the material. If you are using the optional video, move into large group to view the video or turn on the video in the one small group. If you are not viewing the video, you may dismiss with a few introductory words about week 5 and a closing prayer.

Break and return to large group (5 mins.)

View the Video Presentation (50 mins.)

Conclude Session (5 mins.)
- Leader gives a brief response to the video in one or two sentences.
- Leader gives a brief introduction to week 5 in her own words and encourages them toward the completion of their home study.
- Leader closes with prayer. Again, since prayer requests were taken at the beginning of discussion, they would not be necessary at this time.
- Leader takes up name tags as group departs.

AFTER THE SESSION

1. Immediately record any concerns or impressions you had to pray for any member in your group while it is still fresh on your mind. Remember to pray for these throughout the week.

2. Evaluate session 4 by asking yourself the following questions and recording your answers:
   - Was I adequately prepared for today's session?
   - Was I able to begin and end session 4 on time?
   - If not, how can I help to make sure our time is used more wisely in session 5?
   - Do any members need extra encouragement this week? Note whether a card or phone call would be appropriate; then, remember to follow up on each one.
   - What was my overall impression of session 4?

3. Read through "Before the Session" on page 12 so that you will know what preparations you'll need to make before your next session.

JUST BETWEEN US

Beloved Leader, Christ is worthy of your praise! One day you will see His face and hear Him say, "Well done!" You're letting His praises radiate through you as you lead your group to a deeper walk with Christ. You're not just praising Him with your lips. You're praising Him with your whole heart as you make yourself vulnerable through leadership. The life of the apostle Paul should be stimulating plenty of discussion in your group by now! I hope God is giving you glimpses of growth. Leadership offers you the best seat in the house from which to watch God work. May your members see His glorious work in you, too. Thank you for your continued willingness to be a vessel He can use. He is proud of you, Beloved. Believe it.

Notes

_____

_____

_____

_____

_____

_____

_____

_____

_____

_____

_____

_____

SESSION 5
An Unfamiliar Road

BEFORE THE SESSION
Refer to page 12 for a description of session procedures.

Child Care Open, Attendance and Homework Check (15 mins.)

DURING THE SESSION
Large Group—Welcome, Worship, and Prayer (15 mins.)
1. Greet each member as she arrives and give her the name tag she used in the introductory session. Learn to call every participant by name.
2. Lead a time of worship and praise.
3. Pray, asking for God's presence and blessing throughout the session.
4. Dismiss to small groups.

Small Groups (45 mins.)
1. Ask for prayer requests and have prayer. (5 mins.)
2. Review the Week's Principal Questions and Personal Discussion Questions (40 mins.)

Day 1:
- *Principal Question:* How was Paul's visit to Athens particularly unique?
- *Personal Discussion:* As a witness have you also encountered a time when someone responded in any of these three ways? If so, briefly describe the responses.

Day 2:
- *Principal Question:* What was Paul's apparent state of mind when he came to Corinth?
- *Personal Discussion:* What about you? Has God ever used you at a time when you felt weak, with little to offer? If so, when? What happened?

Day 3:
- *Principal Question:* Why did Paul take extra measures to consecrate himself to God in Corinth?
- *Personal Discussion:* When you must face temptation, how can you take extra measures to remain consecrated to God?

Day 4:
- *Principal Question:* How would you describe Apollos?
- *Personal Discussion:* Can you think of a time when an opportunity to serve seemed so rational for you, but you realized later it was not God's will for your life?

Day 5:
- *Principal Question:* What are several extraordinary miracles God performed through Paul in Ephesus?
- *Personal Discussion:* As you conclude today, can you think of a time when God intervened and met with you right at the point of your concern? Describe briefly.

If time allows, ask what ways God spoke directly to members in week 5.

Conclude 40-minute discussion time by affirming your members in their participation today and their apparent grasp of the material. If you are using the optional video, move into large group to view the video or turn on the video in the one small group. If you are not viewing the video, you may dismiss with a few introductory words about week 6 and a closing prayer at this time.

Break and return to large group (5 mins.)

View the Video Presentation (50 mins.)

Conclude Session (5 mins.)
- Leader gives a brief response to the video in one or two sentences.
- Leader gives a brief introduction to week 6 in her own words and encourages them toward the completion of their home study.
- Leader closes with prayer. Again, since prayer requests were taken at the beginning of discussion, they would not be necessary at this time.
- Leader takes up name tags as group departs.

AFTER THE SESSION
1. Immediately record any concerns or impressions you had to pray for any member in your group while it is

still fresh on your mind. Remember to pray for these throughout the week.

2. Evaluate session 5 by asking yourself the following questions and recording your answers:
   - Was I adequately prepared for today's session?
   - Was I able to begin and end session 5 on time?
   - If not, how can I help to make sure our time is used more wisely in session 6?
   - Are there any members that may need extra encouragement this week? Note whether a card or phone call would be appropriate; then, remember to follow up on each one.
   - What was my overall impression of session 5?
3. Read through "Before the Session" on page 12 so that you will know what preparations you'll need to make before your next session.

JUST BETWEEN US

You've hit the halfway point! I hope you're being blessed and challenged. You may also be experiencing difficulties. They don't always wait until we're finished with an important task, do they? Sometimes leaders can feel very isolated and alone in their struggles and losses. Somehow we feel as if we're supposed to always have everything under control. I hope Paul's battles with despair represented the reality that leaders are not immune to feeling defeated. As you continue to serve the flock God has given you, may He cover you with surpassing presence and minister to you in any struggles you might be experiencing. Remember, God always has delivery in mind! May He continue to draw you closer and closer as He develops you into a joyful and effective servant-leader.

Notes

_____

_____

_____

_____

_____

_____

_____

_____

_____

_____

_____

_____

SESSION 6
Travel Ties and Hard Good-byes

BEFORE THE SESSION
Refer to page 12 for a description of session procedures.

Child Care Open, Attendance and Homework Check (15 mins.)

DURING THE SESSION
Large Group—Welcome, Worship, and Prayer (15 mins.)
1. Greet each member as she arrives and give her the name tag she used in the introductory session. Learn to call every participant by name.
2. Lead a time of worship and praise.
3. Pray, asking for God's presence and blessing throughout the session.
4. Dismiss to small groups.

Small Groups (45 mins.)
1. Ask for prayer requests and have prayer. (5 mins.)
2. Review the Week's Principal Questions and Personal Discussion Questions (40 mins.)

Day 1:
- *Principal Question:* What prompted Paul to leave Ephesus?
- *Personal Discussion:* Now think of something you've felt compelled to do in service for Christ. What has burned within your soul? Perhaps completing this sentence will help you discover the answer to this question: God has allowed me to decide to do a number of things for His sake, but beyond all other things I feel I must …

Day 2:
- *Principal Question:* What prompted an eye-opening miracle during one of Paul's long-winded sermons?
- *Personal Discussion:* In what ways have you noticed people today having a shorter attention span than people in the past? What new methods are you using to mature spiritually?

Day 3:
- *Principal Question:* How would you describe the farewell between Paul and the Ephesian elders?
- *Personal Discussion:* These words might evoke one of two responses from you today: You could sense a fresh responsibility for discovering and fulfilling God's tasks for you, OR you may feel a fresh wave of relief that you are not responsible for someone else's task. Which is your response today and why?

Day 4:
- *Principal Question:* Who was Agabus and how did God use him?
- *Personal Discussion:* Have you experienced a time when someone desperately wanted you to do something that you could not do? If so, describe your feelings at the time.

Day 5:
- *Principal Question:* How did Paul fellowship in Christ's sufferings in Jerusalem?
- *Personal Discussion:* How do you need to apply Paul's philosophy of becoming "all things to all men" to save some?

If time allows, ask in what ways God spoke directly to members in week 6.

Conclude 40-minute discussion time by affirming your members in their participation today and their grasp of the material. If you are using the optional video, move into large group to view the video or turn on the video in the one small group. If you are not viewing the videotaped lecture, you may dismiss with a few introductory words about week 7 and a closing prayer.

Break and return to large group (5 mins.)

View the Video Presentation (50 mins.)

Conclude Session (5 mins.)
- Leader gives a brief response to the videotape in one or two sentences.
- Leader gives a brief introduction to week 7 in her own words and encourages them toward the completion of their home study.
- Leader closes with prayer. Again, since prayer requests were taken at the beginning of discussion, they are unnecessary at this time.
- Leader takes up name tags as group departs.

AFTER THE SESSION

1. Immediately record any concerns or impressions you had to pray for any member of your group while it is still fresh on your mind. Remember to pray for these throughout the week.

2. Evaluate session 6 by asking yourself the following questions and recording your answers:
   - Was I adequately prepared for today's session?
   - Was I able to begin and end session 6 on time?
   - If not, how can I help to make sure our time is used more wisely in session 7?
   - Do any members need extra encouragement this week? Note whether a card or phone call would be appropriate; then, remember to follow up on each one.
   - What was my overall impression of session 6?

3. Read through "Before the Session" on page 12 so that you will know what preparations you'll need to make before your next session.

JUST BETWEEN US

Dear Leader, you're already a step ahead! You are actively using your Spiritual gifts and allowing Christ to make Himself conspicuous in you! I praise God for you. Your life is having a significant impact. Don't grow weary in your well doing. God is producing a harvest through your leadership. Reflect on the faces in your group for just a moment. Think about the things we learned in session 6. Thank God for each one of your group members and for all the multi-colored gifts they bring to the body of Christ—then thank Him for our one common bond in all our differences: we have the same Lord!

Notes

SESSION 7
A Walk of Faith

BEFORE THE SESSION
Refer to page 12 for a description of session procedures.

Child Care Open, Attendance and Homework Check (15 mins.)

DURING THE SESSION
Large Group—Welcome, Worship, and Prayer (15 mins.)
1. Greet each member as she arrives and give her the name tag she used in the introductory session. Learn to call every participant by name.
2. Lead a time of worship and praise.
3. Pray, asking for God's presence and blessing throughout the session.
4. Dismiss to small groups.

Small Groups (45 mins.)
1. Ask for prayer requests and have prayer. (5 mins.)
2. Review the Week's Principal Questions and Personal Discussion Questions (40 mins.)

Day 1:
- *Principal Question:* What were several elements of Paul's powerful testimony in Acts 22?
- *Personal Discussion:* Think of someone to whom you really want to witness. What similarities exist between the person and your present or past experiences?

Day 2:
- *Principal Question:* What did you learn about the conscience?
- *Personal Discussion:* Have you discovered a difference since the Holy Spirit became active in your life? If so, describe that difference.

Day 3:
- *Principal Question:* How and why was Paul transported to Caesarea?
- *Personal Discussion:* Have you ever realized the impact of intercessory prayer for your own deliverance? If so, when? Who was praying for you?

Do you think God can deliver us whether or not anyone is praying for us? Assuming your answer was yes, what role do you think prayer plays in someone's deliverance?

Day 4:
- *Principal Question:* What subjects did Paul preach to Felix?
- *Personal Discussion:* Can you think of a time when you heard a very confrontational message which God ultimately used to bring about freedom in your life? What was the general message?

Day 5:
- *Principal Question:* How can a person investigate whether or not Christ is alive today?
- *Personal Discussion:* Reconsider Acts 25:19-21. Throughout our lives we will meet others who are not convinced that Christ is alive. How do you know He's alive? How would you tell an interested but unbelieving person to investigate the living Christ? Name as many ways as you can.

If time allows, ask ways in which God spoke directly to members in week 7.

Conclude 40-minute discussion time by affirming your members in their participation today and their apparent grasp of the material. If you are using the optional video, move into large group to view the video or turn on the video in the one small group. If you are not viewing the video, you may dismiss with a few introductory words about week 8 and a closing prayer.

Break and return to large group (5 mins.)

View the Video Presentation (50 mins.)

Conclude Session (5 mins.)
- Leader gives a brief response to the video in one or two sentences.
- Leader gives a brief introduction to week 8 in her own words and encourages them toward the completion of their home study.
- Leader closes with prayer. Again, since prayer requests were taken at the beginning of discussion, they would not be necessary at this time.
- Leader takes up name tags as group departs.

AFTER THE SESSION

1. Immediately record any concerns or impressions you had to pray for any member of your group while it is still fresh on your mind. Remember to pray for these throughout the week.

2. Evaluate session 7 by asking yourself the following questions and recording your answers:
   - Was I adequately prepared for today's session?
   - Was I able to begin and end session 7 on time?
   - If not, how can I help make sure our time is used more wisely in session 8?
   - Do any members need extra encouragement this week? Note whether a card or phone call would be appropriate; then, remember to follow up.
   - What was my overall impression of session 7?

3. Read through "Before the Session" on page 12 so that you will know what preparations you'll need to make before your next session.

JUST BETWEEN US

Because you've been so faithful to serve God in this capacity and perhaps others, plenty of evidence would exist to convict you of being a Christian if accused! You have a faith that would stand up in court! I hope you're seeing glimpses of growing faith among your members. I pray that God is having His way through His Word and preferences are turning into deep convictions. God desires for the study of Scripture not only to increase our knowledge but to also impact our homes and work places. May the apostle's life challenge all of us to make Christ an intimate part of our daily living. You are setting a wonderful example, my friend. Persevere!

Notes

_____

_____

_____

_____

_____

_____

_____

_____

_____

_____

_____

_____

SESSION 8
The Pathway to Rome

BEFORE THE SESSION
Refer to page 12 for a description of session procedures.

Child Care Open, Attendance and Homework Check (15 mins.)

DURING THE SESSION
Large Group—Welcome, Worship, and Prayer (15 mins.)
1. Greet each member as she arrives and give her the name tag she used in the introductory session. Learn to call every participant by name.
2. Lead a time of worship and praise.
3. Pray, asking for God's presence and blessing throughout the session.
4. Dismiss to small groups.

Small Groups (45 mins.)
1. Ask for prayer requests and have prayer. (5 mins.)
2. Review the Week's Principal Questions and Personal Discussion Questions (40 mins.)

Day 1:
- *Principal Question:* How would you describe Paul's voyage toward Rome?
- *Personal Discussion:* When gentle breezes blow, do you have a tendency to pull up the anchor and ignore your relationship to Christ? If so, what would help your faith become more consistent and less regulated by circumstances?

Day 2:
- *Principal Question:* Why do you think all the passengers' lives were spared?
- *Personal Discussion:* Use your imagination. Can you think of any reasons why the two men might have responded so differently to their commissions?

Day 3:
- *Principal Question:* What did the shipwrecked crew discover while in Malta?
- *Personal Discussion:* Can you think of a time when you were shipwrecked, in a manner of speaking, and encountered unusual kindness?

Day 4:
- *Principal Question:* What ties bind Christians together as brothers and sisters?
- *Personal Discussion:* Have you personally discovered a strong sense of community in the body of Christ? Explain briefly why or why not.

Day 5:
- *Principal Question:* According to the original language, how can a person hear but never understand?
- *Personal Discussion:* Reflect on each original definition once more. How could God use each of these spiritual abilities to enhance your life?

If time allows, ask ways God spoke directly to members in week 8.

Conclude the 40-minute discussion time by affirming your members in their participation today and their apparent grasp of the material. If you are using the optional video, move into large group to view the video or turn on the video in the one small group. If you are not viewing the video, you may dismiss with a few introductory words about week 9 and a closing prayer.

Break and return to large group (5 mins.)

View the Video Presentation (50 mins.)

Conclude Session (5 mins.)
- Leader gives a brief response to the video in one or two sentences.
- Leader gives a brief introduction to week 9 in her own words and encourages them toward the completion of their home study.
- Leader closes with prayer. Again, since prayer requests were taken at the beginning of discussion, they would not be necessary at this time.
- Leader takes up name tags as group departs.

AFTER THE SESSION
1. Immediately record any concerns or impressions you had to pray for any member of your group while it is still fresh on your mind. Remember to pray for these throughout the week.

2. Evaluate session 8 by asking yourself the following questions and recording your answers:
   - Was I adequately prepared for today's session?
   - Was I able to begin and end session 8 on time?
   - If not, how can I help make sure our time is used more wisely in session 9?
   - Are there any members that may need extra encouragement this week? Note whether a card or phone call would be appropriate; then, remember to follow up on each one.
   - What was my overall impression of session 8?
3. Read through "Before the Session" on page 12 so that you will know what preparations you'll need to make before your next session.

JUST BETWEEN US

Beloved Leader, is God's Word continuing to make you a "slave to righteousness"? I hope so! As you give God access to your heart and mind, transformation will take place whether or not you can see it in yourself. I'm a little sad to be leaving the Book of Acts behind. You may be, too. God still has volumes ahead for us! Stay faithful! You've almost completed a very important task. You've accompanied a flock very precious to the Father to a greater intimacy with His Son. Relationships were extremely important to the apostle Paul. He called those whom he served "my joy and crown!" (Phil.4:1). I hope your group has been a joy to you and you to them. Express your appreciation to them often; then listen to the Father whisper His appreciation to you. He loves you so. He appointed you and equipped you for this task. Continue to be teachable and let Him develop you into a mighty servant of God. Only two more weeks to go! Can you believe it! Enjoy.

Notes

_____

_____

_____

_____

_____

_____

_____

_____

_____

_____

_____

SESSION 9
Letters Bridging the Miles

BEFORE THE SESSION
Refer to page 12 for a description of session procedures.

Child Care Open, Attendance and Homework Check (15 mins.)

DURING THE SESSION:
Large Group—Welcome, Worship, and Prayer (15 mins.)
1. Greet each member as she arrives and give her the name tag she used in the introductory session. Learn to call every participant by name.
2. Lead a time of worship and praise.
3. Pray, asking for God's presence and blessing throughout the session.
4. Dismiss to small groups.

Small Groups (45 mins.)
1. Ask for prayer requests and have prayer. (5 mins.)
2. Review the Week's Principal Questions and Personal Discussion Questions (40 mins.)

Day 1:
- *Principal Question:* How can we protect ourselves from being kidnapped by hollow and deceptive philosophy?
- *Personal Discussion:* Name subjects in the Bible that can become a focus or an obsession causing Christians to temporarily lose sight of the Head, Jesus Christ. Can you think of a time when Satan tempted you to misappropriate a biblical concept and prioritize it over Christ? If so, explain.

Day 2:
- *Principal Question:* What are a few things submission does not mean?
- *Personal Discussion:* Stop and pray for an open mind and freedom from the hindrances of negative preconceptions. After you have prayed, read Ephesians 5:21-33.

Day 3:
- *Principal Question:* Which exhortation spoke most clearly to you in your battle against an unseen enemy?

- *Personal Discussion:* The following list includes each of Paul's 14 exhortations about warfare. Evaluate yourself on each of the actions with either a 3 for consistent behaviors, a 2 for need improvement, or a 1 for much improvement needed. Although I encourage you to discuss the test in general you will not need to share your score or specifics in your small group.
___ I realize my natural limitations.
___ I remember (keep in mind) the importance of the full armor.
___ I recognize my real enemies.
___ I realize my enemies' limitations.
___ I retain an active stance.
___ I reject personal hypocrisy.
___ I resist snares of unrighteousness.
___ I remain balanced.
___ I refuse disbelief.
___ I reinforce my mind.
___ I raise my sword.
___ I retain an active prayer life.
___ I remember others in warfare prayer.
___ I specifically remember spiritual leaders in warfare prayer.

___ Total Score

If your score is 34-42, shout Hallelujah! You are presently a well-equipped soldier and an asset to your battalion. Two suggestions: 1) Note exhortations you marked 2 or 1 and ask God to help you become fortified in those areas for your own protection or the protection of your fellow soldiers. 2) Keep up the good work and don't let down your guard! First Corinthians 10:12 applies here!

If your score is 24-33, you have some definite strengths, but you are at risk in several areas. Suggestion: Prioritize becoming more fortified and more effective as a soldier at war. Today's exercise helps you identify strengths and weaknesses so you know where to begin.

If your score is 14-23, shout Help! You are at great risk just like the rest of us have been at one time or another. You are most likely living in painful defeat. Suggestion: Begin praying immediately for God's help and let this be your last day of defeat. "The one who is in you is greater than the one who is in the world!" (1 John 4:4).

Day 4:
- *Principal Question:* How did Paul demonstrate wisdom as he sought reconciliation between Philemon and Onesimus?
- *Personal Discussion:* In what ways did Paul's proposal require Onesimus to humble himself?

Day 5:
- *Principal Question:* What are the thieves of contentment?
- *Personal Discussion:* Have you ever learned to be content in a situation that formerly brought dissatisfaction? If so, how did you finally learn to be content?

If time allows, ask ways in which God spoke directly to members in week 9.

Conclude the 40-minute discussion time by affirming your members in their participation today and their apparent grasp of the material. If you are using the optional video, move into large group to view the video or turn on the video in the one small group. If you are not viewing the video, you may dismiss with a few introductory words about week 10 and a closing prayer at this time.

Break and return to large group (5 mins.)

View the Video Presentation (50 mins.)

Conclude Session (5 mins.)
- Leader gives a brief response to the video in one or two sentences.
- Leader gives a brief introduction to week 10 in her own words and encourages them toward the completion of their home study.
- Leader closes with prayer. Again, since prayer

requests were taken at the beginning of discussion, they would not be necessary at this time.
- Leader takes up name tags as group departs.

AFTER THE SESSION
1. Immediately record any concerns or impressions you had to pray for any member of your group while it is still fresh on your mind. Remember to pray for these throughout the week.
2. Evaluate session 9 by asking yourself the following questions and recording your answers:
   - Was I adequately prepared for today's session?
   - Was I able to begin and end session 9 on time?
   - If not, how can I help make sure our time is used more wisely in session 10?
   - Do any members need extra encouragement this week? Note whether a card or phone call would be appropriate; then, remember to follow up.
   - What was my overall impression of session 9?
3. Read through "Before the Session" on page 12 so that you will know what preparations you'll need to make before your final session.

JUST BETWEEN US

Oh, Beloved, how I pray that the "present and fragmentary knowledge" you've received over the last nine weeks has significantly increased your love for Christ. May your plea echo the apostle Paul's: "I want to know Christ!" May every flock you serve henceforth be directly affected by your journey through the life of one of God's greatest servant-leaders. We are not "apostle Pauls," but we can each share his passion and perseverance. Thank God today for "taking hold" of you and "apprehending" you for His eternal purposes. Please feel special. We are so privileged to serve Him. One day we will suddenly realize what an extreme honor bearing His Name on this earth has been. Just one more week to go. May God touch your heart in a fresh, new way and return you to your group next week with great expectancy for the future.

Notes

S E S S I O N   1 0
Going Home

BEFORE THE SESSION
Refer to page 12 for a description of session procedures.

OPTIONAL: If you might consider leading future Bible study groups and would like to enjoy the benefit of the evaluation of your group, prepare either your own evaluation which you will distribute to your members or one like the example I have included at the end of this leader guide.

Child Care Open, Attendance and Homework Check (15 mins.)

DURING THE SESSION
Large Group—Welcome, Worship, and Prayer (15 mins.)
1. Greet each member as she arrives and give her the name tag she used in the introductory session. Learn to call every participant by name.
2. Lead a time of worship and praise.
3. Pray, asking for God's presence and blessing throughout the session.
4. Dismiss to small groups.

Small Groups (45 mins.)
1. Ask for prayer requests and have prayer. (5 mins.)
2. Review the Week's Principal Questions and Personal Discussion Questions (40 mins.)

Day 1:
• *Principal Question:* How was the apostle Paul able to retain his spiritual passion through so many years and experiences?
• *Personal Discussion:* Why do you think Paul felt this way after all he had been through?

Day 2:
• *Principal Question:* What are several imperatives for strong ministry?
• *Personal Discussion:* Name one of your spiritual gifts and describe the ways you are fanning it into flame.

Day 3:
• *Principal Question:* What are several characteristics of an effective mentor?

• *Personal Discussion:* Even if you are not married, can you think of several ways a wife can also be a friend to her husband?

Day 4:
• *Principal Question:* How did Paul's second imprisonment in Rome differ from his first?
• *Personal Discussion:* If you were in similar conditions and you could only ask for three things (not people), what would they be?

Day 5:
• *Principal Question:* How did Nero's experience in an Olympic race contrast so vividly with Paul's experience in life's most important race?
• *Personal Question:* Do you see anything differently now? If so, explain briefly.

If time allows, ask what ways God spoke directly to members in week 10.

Conclude the 40-minute discussion time by affirming their participation throughout the last 10 weeks and their grasp of material that was often difficult. If you are using the optional video, move into large group to view the last segment or turn on the video in the one small group. If you are not using the video, you may dismiss with concluding remarks and a closing prayer at this time.

Break and return to large group (5 mins.)

View the Video Presentation (50 mins.)

Conclude Session (10 mins. rather than 5, if you are doing an optional evaluation)
• If you prepared an evaluation, pass it out at this time and allow 5 minutes to complete it.
• Leader offers closing remarks to *To Live Is Christ*.
• Leader closes with prayer.
• Leader has a good laugh or a good cry depending on which seems appropriate!

AFTER THE SESSION
1. Evaluate session 10 by asking yourself the following concluding questions and recording your answers:

- Did members seem to grasp the over all principals emphasized in this 10-week study?
- Are there group members with no church home that I should invite to visit church with me?
- Should I remain in contact with any members of my group for the purpose of encouragement?
- Would I consider *taking* another course of this kind?
- Would I consider *leading* another course of this kind?
- What was my overall impression of *To Live Is Christ?*

2. Consider letting us hear from you. If God has spoken to you or done something significant in your life or the lives of one of your members as a direct result of this Bible study, we would love for you to share a brief testimony with us. Write to us, including your name, address, phone number, and church affiliation and mail your testimony to:

LifeWay Church Resources
Dale McCleskey, Editor in Chief
One LifeWay Plaza
Nashville, TN 37234-0175

JUST BETWEEN US

How can I ever thank you, dear friend? I could not do the job God has called me to do through this Bible study without you. I have prayed for you many times and I have asked God to return a bounty of blessing to you far exceeding all you invested. Oh, Believer, He is so worthy. The apostle Paul once said that even when we are faithless, God is faithful. How much more glorious will He be when we offer Him our all? For the rest of your life, may your journey through Acts and your glimpse of the epistles continue to challenge you. May the truths we learned be inscribed on your soul and may the passion of the apostle Paul burn in your heart. Every night when you close your eyes to sleep and meditate over the day behind you, may you be reminded once more that in sickness or in health, in poverty or wealth, enslaved or free: "to live is Christ."

Notes

_____

_____

_____

_____

_____

_____

_____

_____

_____

_____

_____

Evaluation

EXAMPLE EVALUATION FOR LEADERS OF *TO LIVE IS CHRIST*

Group Leader _____ Date _____

Help your group leader in future leader roles by evaluating the following areas. Circle the appropriate letter:

E = Excellent   G = Good   F = Fair   N = Needs Improvement

E - G - F - N   Created an atmosphere of love and acceptance.

E - G - F - N   Was obviously prepared for group sessions.

E - G - F - N   Encouraged group participation.

E - G - F - N   Was supportive to the group.

E - G - F - N   Demonstrated sensitivity to the leadership of the Holy Spirit.

Answer the following:

1.   What did you appreciate most about your group leader?

2.   What suggestions would you like to make to your group leader in leading future Bible Studies?

3.   How do you believe your leader helped enhance your personal experience with this Bible Study?

4.   Did your leader seem to make good use of your time?

5.   What was the most meaningful principle you've learned in this 10-week series?

6.   What additional affirmation do you have for your leader?